INVASIVE SPECIES
LIONFISH

by Alicia Z. Klepeis

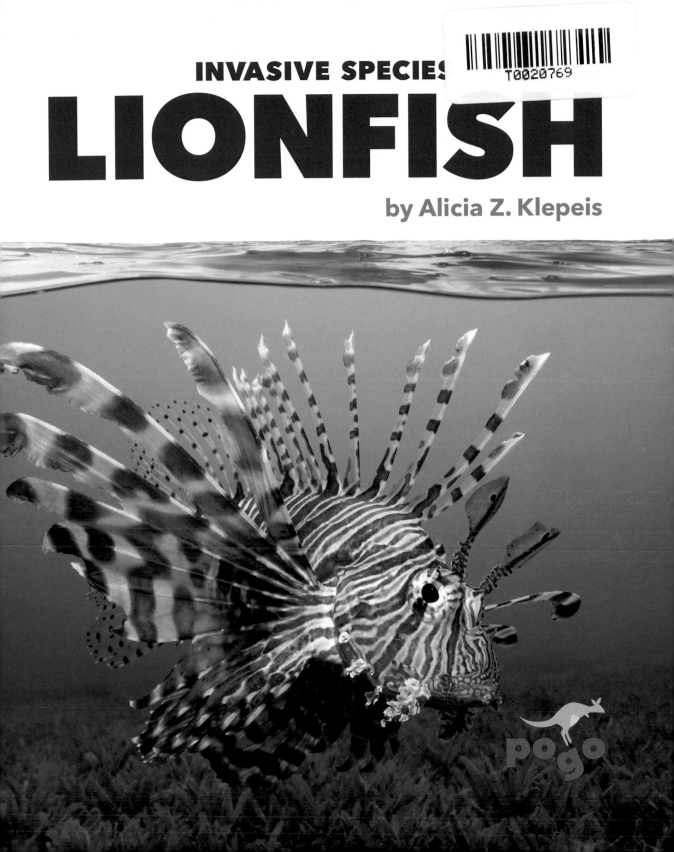

pogo

Ideas for Parents and Teachers

Pogo Books let children practice reading informational text while introducing them to nonfiction features such as headings, labels, sidebars, maps, and diagrams, as well as a table of contents, glossary, and index.

Carefully leveled text with a strong photo match offers early fluent readers the support they need to succeed.

Before Reading

- "Walk" through the book and point out the various nonfiction features. Ask the student what purpose each feature serves.
- Look at the glossary together. Read and discuss the words.

Read the Book

- Have the child read the book independently.
- Invite him or her to list questions that arise from reading.

After Reading

- Discuss the child's questions. Talk about how he or she might find answers to those questions.
- Prompt the child to think more. Ask: When lionfish hunt, they strike fast. Can you name other animals that sneak up on prey?

Pogo Books are published by Jump!
5357 Penn Avenue South
Minneapolis, MN 55419
www.jumplibrary.com

Library of Congress Cataloging-in-Publication Data

Names: Klepeis, Alicia, 1971- author.
Title: Lionfish / by Alicia Z. Klepeis.
Description: Minneapolis: Jump!, Inc., [2023]
Series: Invasive species | Includes index.
Audience: Ages 7-10
Identifiers: LCCN 2022003052 (print)
LCCN 2022003053 (ebook)
ISBN 9781636907987 (hardcover)
ISBN 9781636907994 (paperback)
ISBN 9781636908007 (ebook)
Subjects: LCSH: Pterois miles–Juvenile literature.
Pterois volitans–Juvenile literature. | Introduced fishes–Juvenile literature.
Classification: LCC QL638.S42 K54 2023 (print) | LCC QL638.S42 (ebook) | DDC 597/.68–dc23/eng/20220126
LC record available at https://lccn.loc.gov/2022003052
LC ebook record available at https://lccn.loc.gov/2022003053

Editor: Eliza Leahy
Designer: Michelle Sonnek

Photo Credits: Eric Isselee/Shutterstock, cover; Laura Dts/Shutterstock, 1, 4; Drew McArthur/Shutterstock, 3; Rich Carey/Shutterstock, 5; Keat Eung/Shutterstock, 6-7tl; Natalie Robson/iStock, 6-7tr; Reinhard Dirscherl/Alamy, 6-7bl, 18, 19; Anna segeren/Shutterstock, 6-7br; Tran Thu Hang/Shutterstock, 8 (shoreline); imageBROKER/Alamy, 8 (ocean); alexkoral/Shutterstock, 9; Minden Pictures/SuperStock, 10-11; Michael Grana/Shutterstock, 12-13; F1online digitale Bildagentur GmbH/Alamy, 14-15 (lionfish); Michael Patrick O'Neill/Alamy, 14-15 (crab); Stephen Frink Collection/Alamy, 16-17; Peter Leahy/Shutterstock, 20-21; Piyatida Tepphitak/Shutterstock, 23.

Printed in the United States of America at Corporate Graphics in North Mankato, Minnesota.

TABLE OF CONTENTS

CHAPTER 1

FANCY FINS

What fish has fancy fins and 18 sharp spines? It is a lionfish! This fish has stripes. They are white and brown or dark red.

◄······ spine

A lionfish has many fins to help it swim. When the fins spread out, they look like a lion's mane. That is how this fish got its name!

fin

Lionfish are **native** to the Indian and Pacific Oceans. They can live in many **habitats**. They are often found near **coral reefs**.

Others live in **seagrass beds** or **mangrove forests**. Some live among **shipwrecks**!

DID YOU KNOW?

Lionfish can be up to 19 inches (48 centimeters) long. They can weigh almost four pounds (1.8 kilograms).

coral reef

seagrass bed

mangrove forest

shipwreck

CHAPTER 2

SPREADING OUT

Lionfish are an **invasive species** in the Atlantic Ocean. They were first seen near Florida's coast in 1985. While all oceans are connected, species usually stay in one area. So how did lionfish get to the Atlantic?

Lionfish are popular pets. People keep them in fish tanks. Scientists think people may have released pet lionfish into the Atlantic Ocean.

Lionfish spread quickly in the Atlantic. How? They **reproduce** often. Adult female lionfish can lay 2 million eggs each year! This keeps their **population** growing.

lionfish eggs

TAKE A LOOK!

Lionfish usually live in warm ocean waters. Where have they been found in the Atlantic Ocean? Take a look!

UNITED STATES

ATLANTIC OCEAN

GULF OF MEXICO

CARIBBEAN SEA

■ = lionfish invasive range

N
W ✛ E
S

Lionfish have few **predators** in the Atlantic. Why? It may be because their unusual look scares off possible predators. They also have **venom** in their spines. It poisons animals that get too close. Without many predators, the lionfish population increases.

DID YOU KNOW?

Lionfish spines poke predators that try to attack. This is how venom gets in them.

spine

crab

Lionfish cause problems in their new homes. They eat the same foods as native fish. These foods include crabs, shrimp, and **mollusks**.

Lionfish sneak up on **prey**. They use their large fins to corner it. Then, they strike. *Gulp!*

DID YOU KNOW?

A lionfish's stomach can stretch 30 times its normal size. This helps the fish eat prey more than half its size!

Lionfish eat parrotfish and other **herbivores** that live on coral reefs. These animals keep coral reefs healthy. How? They eat the **algae** that grow on the reefs. Without parrotfish, algae can grow over the reefs. This can kill the coral.

parrotfish

CHAPTER 3

CATCHING LIONFISH

People are working to stop the spread of lionfish. But it is hard. Scuba divers try to catch the fish. They use spears. Some divers sell the fish for people to eat. There is even a saying: "Eat 'em to beat 'em."

spear

Scientists study lionfish. They study what they eat and how they harm their new homes. This helps scientists figure out where the fish could spread next.

Lionfish are fantastic fish. But the Atlantic Ocean is not their natural home. Native fish and other ocean wildlife will live better without them.

ACTIVITIES & TOOLS

NATIVE FISH IN YOUR AREA

Native fish are an important part of the food web. Learn about the native fish in your area in this activity!

What You Need:
- a computer, books, or magazines
- sheets of paper
- colored pencils, markers, or crayons
- tape or glue
- posterboard or a large sheet of paper

❶ **Use a computer, books, or magazines to learn about native fish species in your area. Choose two.**

❷ **Find out what the fish look like and how large they get.**

❸ **On a sheet of paper, draw one of the fish. Write down how big it gets.**

❹ **Repeat Step 3 for the other fish.**

❺ **Tape or glue your drawings to your posterboard.**

❻ **What are some differences between the native fish you researched and lionfish? Are there any similarities?**

GLOSSARY

algae: Small plants without roots or stems that grow mainly in water.

coral reefs: Long lines of coral that lie in warm, shallow waters.

habitats: The places where animals or plants are usually found.

herbivores: Animals that eat plants.

invasive species: Any kind of living organism that is not native to a specific area.

mangrove forests: Coastal swamps that flood at high tide and contain trees or shrubs that have tangled roots above the ground.

mollusks: Animals with soft bodies and hard shells that live in water or damp habitats.

native: Growing or living naturally in a particular area of the world.

population: The total number of living things in a certain area.

predators: Animals that hunt other animals for food.

prey: Animals that are hunted by other animals for food.

reproduce: To produce offspring.

seagrass beds: Areas of the ocean floor where marine plants grow in groups, providing habitat for many animals.

shipwrecks: The remains of ships that have sunk at sea.

venom: Poison produced by some animals, usually passed into a victim's body by a bite or sting.

INDEX

TO LEARN MORE

Finding more information is as easy as 1, 2, 3.

❶ Go to www.factsurfer.com

❷ Enter "lionfish" into the search box.

❸ Choose your book to see a list of websites.

FACT SURFER